LIN ★ MANUEL
MIRANDA

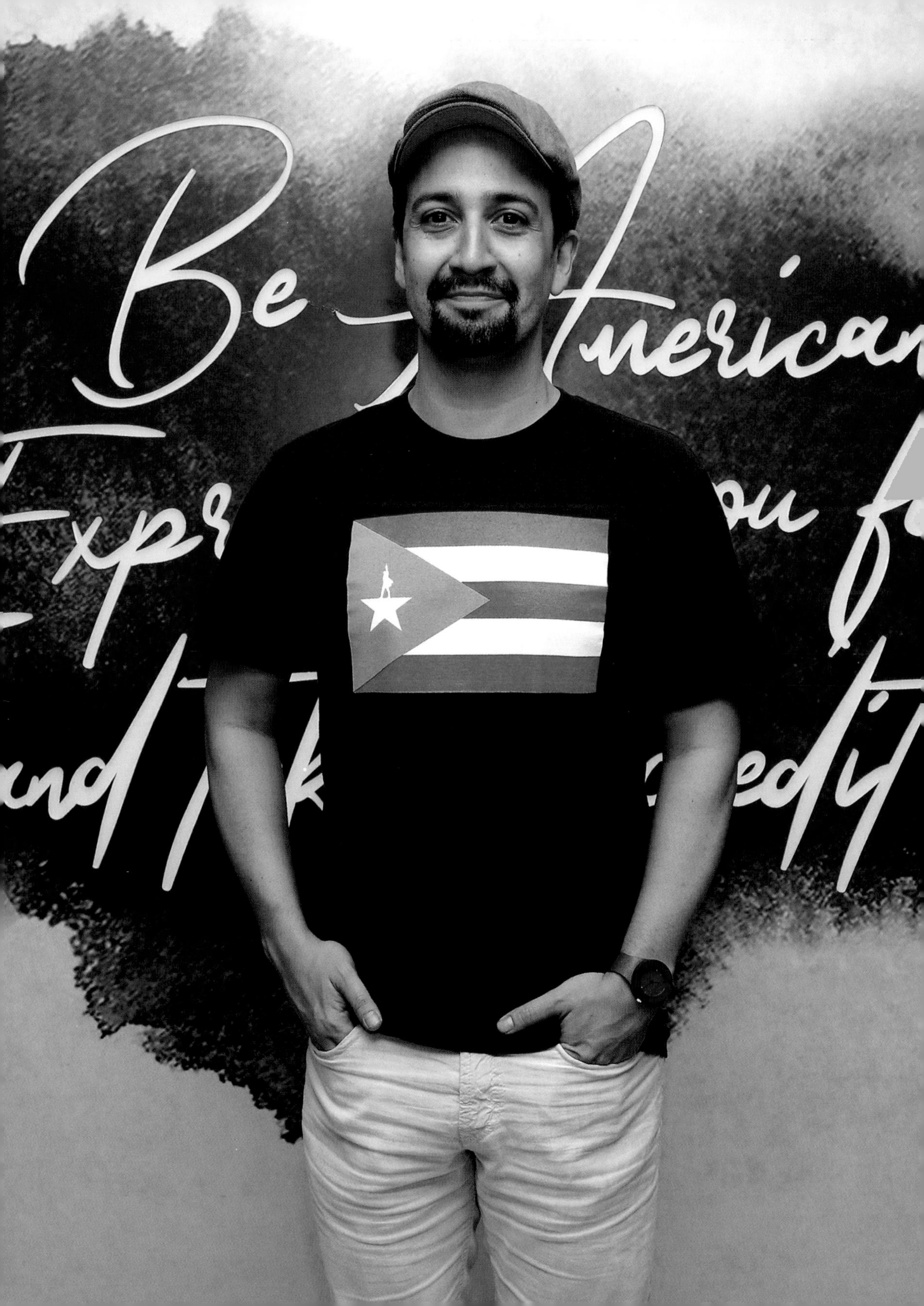

LIN ★ MANUEL MIRANDA

Revolutionary PLAYWRIGHT, COMPOSER, AND ACTOR

HEATHER E. SCHWARTZ

LERNER PUBLICATIONS ◆ MINNEAPOLIS

Lerner Publications Company
An imprint of Lerner Publishing Group, Inc.
241 First Avenue North
Minneapolis, MN 55401 USA

For reading levels and more information, look up this title at www.lernerbooks.com.

Image credits: Alexander Tamargo/Getty Images, p. 2; CBS Photo Archive/Getty Images, p. 6; Corbis Entertainment/Getty Images, p. 8; Sylvain Gaboury/Patrick McMullan/Getty Images, p. 9; StockAB/Alamy Stock Photo, p. 13; Bruce Glikas/Getty Images, p. 15; Mario Tama/Getty Images, p. 16; Neilson Barnard/Getty Images, pp. 17, 27; Carolyn Cole/Getty Images, p. 18; Theo Wargo/ Getty Images, p. 19; JIMI CELESTE/Patrick McMullan/Getty Images, p. 20; GL Archive/Alamy Stock Photo, p. 21; WENN Rights Ltd/Alamy Stock Photo, p. 23; Pictorial Press Ltd/Alamy Stock Photo, p. 24; John Lamparski/WireImage/Getty Images, p. 25; Walter McBride/WireImage/Getty Images, pp. 28, 29; Kevin Mazur/Getty Images, p. 30; John Paul Filo/CBS/Getty Images, p. 31; EDUARDO MUNOZ ALVAREZ/AFP/Getty Images, p. 32; Alberto E. Rodriguez/Getty Images, p. 33; LUCAMAR PRODUCTIONS/MARC PLATT PRODUCTIONS/WALT DISNEY/Album/Alamy Stock Photo, p. 34; Anadolu Agency/Getty Images, p. 35; Gladys Vega/Getty Images, pp. 36, 38; NICHOLAS KAMM/AFP/Getty Images, p. 37.

Cover Images: photo one/Shutterstock.com; Frazer Harrison/Getty Images.

Design Element: photo one/Shutterstock.com.

Main body text set in Rotis Serif Std 55 Regular. Typeface provided by Adobe Systems.

Library of Congress Cataloging-in-Publication Data

Names: Schwartz, Heather E., author.
Title: Lin-Manuel Miranda : revolutionary playwright, composer, and actor / Heather E. Schwartz.
Description: Minneapolis : Lerner Publications, [2020] | Series: Gateway biographies | Audience: Ages 9–14. | Audience: Grades 4–6. | Includes bibliographical references and index.
Identifiers: LCCN 2019002743 (print) | LCCN 2019013398 (ebook) | ISBN 9781541556188 (eb pdf) | ISBN 9781541556164 (lb : alk. paper) | ISBN 9781541574335 (pb :alk. paper)
Subjects: LCSH: Miranda, Lin-Manuel, 1980-–Juvenile literature. | Actors–United States– Biography–Juvenile literature. | Composers–United States–Biography–Juvenile literature. | Lyricists–United States–Biography–Juvenile literature.
Classification: LCC PN2287.M6446 (ebook) | LCC PN2287.M6446 S39 2020 (print) | DDC 792.02/8092 [B] —dc23

LC record available at https://lccn.loc.gov/2019002743

Manufactured in the United States of America
1-46072-43488-5/7/2019

Contents

Lin-Manuel Miranda's Broadway musicals have garnered many Tony Awards. Here he is accepting one of the eleven Tonys won by *Hamilton* in 2016.

Standing on the stage at the 2016 Tony Awards was a proud moment for Lin-Manuel Miranda. He had just won the award for Best Original Score. But Miranda was never one to focus only on himself and his accomplishments. His artistry was genius, but he was also there that night because he'd worked hard to tell someone else's story.

A recent mass shooting in Orlando was all over the news. When the time came for Miranda's acceptance speech, he took his chance to speak to people's pain, reciting a sonnet he had written:

When senseless acts of tragedy remind us
That nothing here is promised, not one day.
This show is proof that history remembers
We lived through times when hate and fear seemed stronger;
We rise and fall and light from dying embers,
remembrances that hope and love last longer
And love is love is love is love is love is love is love is love
cannot be killed or swept aside.

He ended with a quick thank-you, leaving the microphone as the audience cheered and applauded for the creator of the year's most revolutionary musical, *Hamilton*.

Sounds of Childhood

Lin-Manuel Miranda's childhood was a symphony of sounds. Born January 16, 1980, in New York City, he grew up listening to different kinds of music and discovering what moved him. His parents, Luz Towns-Miranda, a clinical psychologist, and Luis A. Miranda Jr., a political consultant, filled their home with Latin music from their native Puerto Rico, where Lin-Manuel spent his summers. They also loved the Broadway show tunes that sprang from their new city. Although they couldn't afford

Miranda and his parents, Luz and Luis, still love attending musicals on Broadway together.

Miranda's sister (*left*) helped her little brother with his early musical endeavors.

to see every show live, they collected recordings from their favorites, including *Camelot* and *The Unsinkable Molly Brown*. Lin-Manuel did get to attend a few Broadway shows: *Les Misérables*, *Cats*, and *The Phantom of the Opera*. He also listened to songs from *Jesus Christ Superstar* and *Man of La Mancha* over and over—as many times as he liked.

Pop, hip-hop, and rap also permeated Lin-Manuel's world. He had an older sister, Luz (now Luz Miranda-Crespo), whose taste in music he admired. When the time came for his stage debut—lip-synching in the kindergarten talent show at Hunter College Elementary School—Luz helped him memorize the words to "Land of Confusion" by Genesis. She dressed him in a Benetton sweater and sent him off to wow the crowd.

During rides to school, Lin-Manuel learned more lyrics from his bus driver, who was into rap bands such as

Boogie Down Productions, Geto Boys, and the Sugarhill Gang. Lin-Manuel also studied piano and played in his first recital when he was about six. After his first song, he was inspired by the applause from the audience. He played another. More applause encouraged him further. He kept playing until the teacher had to step in so that another student could get a turn.

When Lin-Manuel was nine, the movie *The Little Mermaid* came out. He was blown away. "I went and saw it three times in the theater. Then I dragged my parents back and my family back to see it a couple of more times," he said. "I don't know why it changed my life as much as it did. I think Sebastian the crab had a big amount to do with it. The fact that this calypso number happens under the water just knocked my socks off when I was a kid. It had, like, this power over me. I would perform that thing. I would jump up on my desk in fourth grade and sing that song."

By sixth grade, Lin-Manuel didn't have to use his desk as a stage anymore. He began performing in school musicals, which were mini versions of full-length shows. He had parts in *The Wiz, Oklahoma!, Fiddler on the Roof, West Side Story, Peter Pan*, and *Bye Bye Birdie.* For one performance, Edmunda Claudio—a close family friend who lived with Lin-Manuel's family and helped to raise him—even made him a fancy gold lamé jacket to wear as a costume. The number required his female classmates to pretend to be in love with him. He loved every minute of it.

Edmunda Claudio

In addition to his parents and sister, Lin-Manuel grew up with Edmunda Claudio, an older woman who was like a grandmother to him. In fact, Lin-Manuel even called her his Abuela Mundi. *Abuela* means "grandmother" in Spanish. Edmunda Claudio had been Lin-Manuel's father's nanny when he was growing up. She raised him in Puerto Rico. After Lin-Manuel was born, she joined Lin-Manuel's parents in the United States.

One of Lin-Manuel's earliest memories is of walking and holding hands with Abuela Mundi on a city street when he was three years old. They entered a bodega (market) together and went to the back, where they knew there were slot machines. Lin-Manuel pulled a slot machine lever for his abuela, hoping for good luck as he listened to merengue music playing in the background.

Artist under Development

After elementary school, Lin-Manuel attended Hunter College High School in New York from grades 7–12. The school's theater program was student run, and Lin-Manuel continued acting. But his interests led him to do even more. He started writing his own one-act plays and musicals. He also jumped into the role of director while he was a student.

"When you are directing your fellow high school students, and you have no authority to pay, fire, or punish them, no motivating force at all other than to make them believe in your vision of how the show should be, you learn to project confidence very quickly," he said.

After graduating from high school, Miranda went on to Wesleyan University in Middletown, Connecticut, where he majored in theater. While studying acting and directing, he also learned how to apply makeup, do the lighting for shows, paint sets, and create costumes. He focused much of his attention on sound design and writing music. Miranda was happy to learn about all aspects of the theater. It helped him understand how everyone works together to create a show.

Theater wasn't all he studied at Wesleyan. But even during other classes, Miranda's mind tended to wander to the stage. One day during astronomy, in his sophomore year, he scribbled the words "In the Heights" in his notebook. It was an idea he had for another show he wanted to write.

Wasting no time, Miranda wrote one song for his show and applied to Wesleyan's Second Stage program, which is a student-run theater company. He was accepted and given access to a space. All he had to do was come up with a full-length show in just a few months' time.

"I barely slept, I barely ate. I just wrote," he recalls. "I put in all the things I'd always wanted to see onstage: propulsive freestyle rap scenes outside of bodegas, salsa numbers that also revealed character and story. I tried to write the kind of show I'd want to be in."

When he was finished, he had an eighty-minute show that included fourteen original songs. The story focused on a love triangle set in Washington Heights, a neighborhood in the Manhattan borough of New York City. Although it wasn't a true story, Miranda drew from some of his own background, growing up in a nearby neighborhood. Living in a house for Latino students that year, he felt very connected to his cultural roots.

The setting and inspiration for Miranda's musical *In the Heights* was a neighborhood like this one in Washington Heights.

The show ran at the Patricelli '92 Theater on campus for three days in April 2000. "Two remarkable things happened," Miranda said. "One, we broke box-office records for the '92 Theater that year—it was insanity. Two, I was approached by [a senior]. He loved the show and said, 'My friends and I are starting a production company when we graduate, and we want to help you bring it to New York.' I said, 'That sounds awesome,' and went to the cast party and promptly forgot about his offer."

Rewriting and Revising

Throughout college, Miranda wrote another musical and three one-act plays. His first job in his field was a summer internship at Repertorio Español, an off-Broadway theater in New York City. It wasn't glamorous work. He didn't produce and star in shows. He didn't even get paid.

"I mostly cleaned floors and struck sets, but I got to see amazing theater for free," he said.

For his senior thesis, or final written project, Miranda wrote an original musical called *On Borrowed Time*. The student who'd loved *In the Heights*, Thomas Kail, hadn't forgotten about Miranda and came back to campus to see it in 2002. By then Kail had started the production company Back House Productions with his friends Neil Stewart, John Mailer, and Anthony Veneziale.

Miranda with collaborator Thomas Kail (*left*).

After graduating from college, Miranda met with Back House Productions at their small Manhattan theater. They wanted to work with him to develop *In the Heights* as a bigger show. Miranda listened to Kail's ideas and realized that his musical could be even better.

"Two thoughts occur to me. The first is: "This guy is smarter and understands the show better than anyone I've ever met." The second is: "I have to completely rewrite this show," he said.

He was out of college, so Miranda had to support himself. He held a day job teaching seventh-grade English at Hunter College High School, and on the side, he wrote music for political ads. He got the political gigs through his father's work as a political consultant. Miranda's father encouraged his son to go to law school. But he supported Miranda's decision to stick with theater and wanted to help in any way he could.

"As parents, you help in both big and small ways," his father said. "When he talks about fundraising for *In the Heights*, he remembers our allowing him to raid our refrigerator so that he didn't have to buy food and letting him empty his mom's closet so that he could have a garage sale."

Miranda revisited his high school alma mater, Hunter College High School, when he taught seventh-grade English there after college.

Although Luis Miranda (*left*) originally wanted his son to become a lawyer, he supported Lin-Manuel's desire to pursue his theatrical dreams and was happy to help him.

Miranda's revisions went well, but the process was slow. As the show morphed and changed, Back House Productions held readings for audiences. With each reading, interest grew. A few Broadway producers attended and liked what they saw. But the show still wasn't ready yet. Over the next few years, Miranda continued to work on the story, the songs, and his performance.

Eventually, the show was performed in workshop form at a few theaters. In 2007 it was finally ready for a full production at an off-Broadway theater. By then it was almost completely different from Miranda's original work. The lyrics and melodies in his songs were all new. An important new character had been added. A Cuban immigrant who loved playing the lottery, Abuela Claudia was modeled after Miranda's Abuela Mundi.

Miranda was proud, however, that he did not change his original story. He believed all along that it was important to portray a realistic Latino character, one who did not buy into stereotypes and clichés. With *In the Heights*, he told the story he wanted to tell.

"Anytime I've seen Washington Heights in a movie, there's always a drug deal taking place. And there have been two Broadway musicals that have featured Puerto Ricans prominently—*West Side Story* and *The Capeman*—and both of them have gang members in the '50s with knives," he said. "The overwhelming majority of residents

Miranda looked very much at home on the set of the Tony Award–winning *In the Heights*, which he wrote and starred in.

in Washington Heights are not involved with crime or drugs. It would be inauthentic for me to write about drug deals and domestic abuse. It wasn't my experience."

Broadway Bound

By the time *In the Heights* was finished, Miranda had been working on the show for eight years. When it opened at the Richard Rodgers Theatre on Broadway on March 9, 2008, audiences loved it. That year the show won four Tony Awards, including awards for Best Musical and Best Original Score. Miranda used his acceptance speech to thank his parents and his girlfriend, Vanessa Nadal, a dancer, scientist, and attorney.

Miranda wowed the audience at the Tony Awards in 2008 by performing a rap as his acceptance speech.

Miranda beams with his future wife, Vanessa Nadal, by his side.

"Vanessa, who still leaves me breathless, thanks for loving me when I was broke and making breakfast," he said, in an acceptance rap onstage at the Tony Awards.

Although Miranda was busy with his Broadway show, he found time for a vacation later that year. Heading to Mexico with Nadal, he brought along a book to read. *Alexander Hamilton* by Ron Chernow was 832 pages long. Miranda was moved by the story of one of the United States' founders. He kept thinking about it long after he'd finished the book.

"As I'm reading the book it was one of those rare experiences where I was also picturing it," he said. "Alexander Hamilton was someone who on the strength of his words and ideas pulled himself from

Alexander Hamilton, a founder of the United States of America

unbelievably humble circumstances to the top of the nation. Then he sort of destroyed that good will as he continued to fight and continued to believe he was the smartest guy in the room."

In early 2009, Miranda worked on another show that tapped into his Latino roots. *West Side Story* focused on Puerto Ricans but told their story in English. Miranda translated scenes and songs into Spanish to make the show more authentic before it hit Broadway.

Meanwhile, in May that year, the White House invited Miranda along with other artists to perform for an evening of poetry and music. Miranda came back to his interest in Hamilton. When he told the audience that he was working on an album about someone who he thought "embodies hip-hop, Treasury Secretary Alexander Hamilton," the audience laughed. But when he began performing his rap about Hamilton that told the story of the first twenty years of his life, the faces in the audience lit up with delight. President Barack Obama and First Lady Michelle Obama were riveted. At the end, the crowd cheered him with a standing ovation.

During 2010 Miranda cowrote the score to the musical *Bring It On* and started working to make *In the Heights* into a movie. He also kept plugging away at his album about Hamilton. But work wasn't all Miranda focused on that year.

On September 5, Miranda married Nadal at the Belvedere Mansion in Staatsburg, New York. He planned a surprise during the reception, where Broadway singers—who were among the guests—serenaded the bride with a song from the musical *Fiddler on the Roof*. Nadal couldn't hide her shock, but she smiled happily too. Since early in their relationship, Miranda had known she was the one for him. With Nadal, he could always be himself, whether celebrating or hard at work creating his art.

"I look like a crazy person on the subway when I'm writing," he said. "I sing and run around. I pace a lot. I need to move. But I wasn't at all self-conscious around her."

Miranda joined the cast of *In the Heights* for two weeks before the show closed its run on Broadway on January 9, 2011. It was an ending for Miranda. But it was also a time of new beginnings. By now, he was a well-known and respected artist with plenty of projects in the works.

The cast of *In the Heights* celebrates on the final night of the musical's successful run on Broadway.

In Demand

One year later, in 2012, Miranda took the stage at Lincoln Center in New York City to rap sections of "The Hamilton Mixtape," his collection of songs about Alexander Hamilton. He was still working on it but couldn't say no to a performance date that happened to fall on Hamilton's birthday, January 11.

In February, Miranda joined the cast of *Merrily We Roll Along* at the New York City Center, playing the role of a songwriter in a Broadway musical. That same month,

Miranda made his film debut playing Reggie in *The Odd Life of Timothy Green*.

he had a small role in *The Odd Life of Timothy Green*, a Disney movie. By the following year, he had a much stronger relationship with Disney.

In the winter of 2013, he sent the company a six-song demo and interviewed for a job writing songs for the movie *Moana*. He used his demo to show that he could work with different languages, since he knew that Samoan would be important in the film. Months passed, but he finally learned that he got the job.

All the while, Miranda stayed busy working on his *Hamilton* project. What began as a collection of songs had become a script for an entire show. Miranda worked

Ron Chernow, author of the biography of Alexander Hamilton

hard to tell the story accurately. He read Alexander Hamilton's published works and visited historic sites of the Revolutionary War in New York City. Ron Chernow, the author of the book that inspired Miranda, became his historical consultant.

"He tries first to stick to the facts, and if he has to deviate from the facts, I have found that there is always a very good reason for him doing it," Chernow said. "I said to him, 'Do you want me to tell you when I see historical errors?' And he said, 'Absolutely. I want the historians to respect this.'"

In 2014 Miranda's family grew with the birth of his first son on November 10. The child's proud parents named him Sebastian. Miranda announced his arrival in the style of a script on Twitter: "[The screams reach a frenzied pitch. SEBASTIAN MIRANDA enters. He is 7 pounds 10 ounces.] End Of Act One."

Meanwhile, Miranda struggled with a section of his script about Alexander Hamilton. He planned to write a song about Hamilton's death, but it wasn't coming. On New Year's Day, he took an early morning walk to think and write without disturbance. Twenty-four hours later, he had a poem instead. Without music behind them, the words were even more powerful in expressing Hamilton's last thoughts and feelings.

Miranda spent seven years writing *Hamilton*. He labored over it to try to offer something the world had never seen before. "Unless I express it, it's only going to stay in my brain," he said. "If I don't get this idea out of my head and onto paper, it dies with me."

Taking His Time

Miranda was in no hurry when he started working on *Hamilton*. He took a year to write the first song, "Alexander Hamilton," which told the founder's story based on the first forty pages of Ron Chernow's book. Then he worked on his next song, "My Shot," for a year before it was finished. He wanted every song to have the perfect lyrics.

Miranda needed to pick up the pace if he wanted to see his work reach the stage, however. Eventually, Thomas Kail, who'd worked with him on *In the Heights*, encouraged him to write faster. Miranda wrote wherever he happened to be. He wrote "You'll Be Back" on his honeymoon, and "Wait for It" while riding the subway to a friend's party in Brooklyn.

Hamilton

Hamilton was on its way to becoming Miranda's second Broadway show. First, however, it was performed in preview shows in January 2015 at the off-Broadway Public Theater in New York. It officially premiered at that theater on February 17.

On August 6, 2015, *Hamilton* opened on Broadway at the Richard Rodgers Theatre. Miranda played the title role, and he filled the cast with African American, Latino, and Asian actors. That surprised some people, who expected to see the United States' founders portrayed by white actors. But Miranda was quick to defend his choice.

"Let's not pretend this is a textbook. Let's make the founders of our country look like what our country looks like now. We are every shade and every color," he said.

The racially diverse cast of *Hamilton* included Leslie Odom (*left*). Odom played Aaron Burr, a white man in real life and the man who shot Hamilton in a duel.

The cast soaks up the applause for their smash hit on *Hamilton*'s opening night in August 2015.

Hamilton was an immediate success. Audiences and critics loved it. One *New York Times* critic said of the show: "*Hamilton* is making its own resonant history by changing the language of musicals. And it does so by insisting that the forms of song most frequently heard on pop radio stations in recent years—rap, hip-hop, R&B ballads—have both the narrative force and the emotional interiority to propel a hefty musical about long-dead white men whose solemn faces glower from the green bills in our wallets."

In September 2015, Miranda received a MacArthur Fellowship (known unofficially as a genius grant) from the MacArthur Foundation for his work on *Hamilton*. The award included a $625,000 prize paid out over five years. The following year, *Hamilton* won another prestigious honor, the 2016 Pulitzer Prize in Drama, given to only eight other musicals throughout the last century.

Miranda was quick to use his success to give back. In October 2015, he worked with partners to create the Hamilton Education Program. It was ultimately expanded to run through 2020 so that 250,000 students could learn

Miranda enjoys a moment with students backstage who attended a performance of *Hamilton* as part of the Hamilton Education Program. Giving back to his community is important to Miranda.

about the history told in *Hamilton* and then visit the theater to see the show. The students also had the chance to learn about how Miranda wrote his songs and to work on their own performance pieces.

For the 2016 Tony Awards in June, *Hamilton* broke the record by being nominated for sixteen awards. The show won for Best Musical, Best Actor in a Musical, Best Featured Actor in a Musical, Best Featured Actress in a Musical, Best Direction of a Musical, Best Choreography,

Hamilton received the Tony Award for Best Musical in 2016, along with many other awards.

With *Hamilton*'s success assured, Miranda (*far right*) was ready to strike out in new directions and left his role in *Hamilton* soon after the show swept the Tony Awards.

Best Book, Best Orchestrations, Best Costume Design of a Musical, Best Lighting Design of a Musical, and Best Original Score. Taking home eleven awards, the show was just one shy of the record set by *The Producers*, which won twelve Tonys.

A month later, Miranda left the cast of *Hamilton*. He was already at work on other projects, including preparing for his role in the movie *Mary Poppins Returns*. However, leaving his *Hamilton* role didn't mean leaving the show entirely behind. He said he would come back to that role in the future. And he dreamed of one day taking the show to Puerto Rico.

Speaking Out

Hamilton was almost universally celebrated. In late 2016, however, the show made headlines for a controversial reason. On November 8, Donald Trump was pronounced the next president of the United States in an election that sharply divided the country. Many felt that Trump did not represent America's diverse population. The cast of *Hamilton* was among those who worried about representation for people of color, immigrants, gay people, women, and other groups.

On November 18, Trump's vice president, Mike Pence, went to see *Hamilton* with his wife. Spotted in the audience, he was booed by many people. After the show, cast member Brandon Dixon spoke to the audience, addressing Pence as well before he left.

"There's nothing to boo here, ladies and gentlemen. There's nothing to boo here. We're all here sharing a story of love. We have a message for you, sir. We hope that you will hear us out," Dixon said. "We, sir, are the diverse America who are alarmed and anxious that your new administration will not protect us, our planet, our children, our parents—or defend us and uphold our inalienable rights, sir. But we truly hope that this show has inspired you to uphold our American values and work on behalf of *all* of us. All of us."

The cast of *Hamilton* hoped that Vice President Pence would embrace their call for unity amidst diversity.

Moving On and Moving Forward

At the end of 2016, Disney released the movie *Moana*, featuring Miranda's original songs, including "How Far I'll Go." Early in 2017, Miranda rapped an introduction to the song at the Oscars, where it was nominated for Best Original Song. Although the song didn't win, it was a milestone moment as Miranda's first Oscar nomination.

Dwayne "The Rock" Johnson (*left*) voiced the character of Maui in *Moana*. He and Miranda performed one of the film's songs together for its world premiere in Hollywood.

Miranda enjoyed playing the role of Jack in *Mary Poppins Returns* and said it let him get in touch with his inner child.

During the summer of 2017, Miranda spent time in London filming *Mary Poppins Returns*. He released an instrumental version of the *Hamilton* album. And he attended the opening of that show in Los Angeles. Then a natural disaster sent his work in a new direction.

On September 20, Hurricane Maria hit Puerto Rico. The storm's 155-mile-an-hour (249 km) winds uprooted trees, destroyed homes, and knocked out power. The entire island was devastated. Miranda was devastated too. He had family there and knew the island well from spending so much time there as a child. He was deeply offended by Trump's tweets that seemed to criticize the hurricane victims instead of offering support and relief.

As a respected and well-known artist, Miranda could speak out and reach people himself. He could also take action. He responded on Twitter and wrote a song called "Almost Like Praying" to raise money for Puerto Rico. He recorded it with multiple well-known Latin musical artists. By November he had a big announcement: he was

Hurricane Maria upended the lives of millions of people.

Puerto Rico's recovery will take a long time, but Miranda is committed to helping. On this occasion, he and his father delivered food to victims.

taking *Hamilton* to Puerto Rico and would reprise his leading role. He wanted the opening, in January 2019, to send the message that the island and its people would come back from the tragedy.

"The road to recovery in Puerto Rico is not a simple one nor is it one that relies solely on aid from the American government on the mainland," Miranda said. "Together, we will cultivate, fund, and execute practical and actionable solutions to kick-start and continue the island's road to recovery for years to come."

Always remembering his roots, Miranda had grown from a talented young boy into an artist and activist.

His world continued to expand with the birth of his second son, Francisco, on December 11, 2017. He ended the year with another announcement for fans: the launch of HamilDrops, a series of new *Hamilton*-related content released throughout 2018. Former president Barack Obama performed a spoken part in one of these pieces.

January 2018 kicked off a whirlwind year for Miranda. Hamilton set off on tour, including three weeks in Puerto Rico, where he reprised the title role. Throughout the year, Miranda was a sought-after star in other productions too. He joined the cast of a BBC show. He announced plans to compose songs for an animated feature and direct a musical called *Tick, Tick . . . Boom!*

President Barack Obama loved the show *Hamilton* and even performed in a related endeavor called HamilDrops.

Staging *Hamilton* in Puerto Rico raised millions of dollars for relief efforts.

Some of Miranda's biggest news that year concerned his own first musical, *In the Heights*, and his continued efforts to help Puerto Rico. In May, Warner Bros. announced plans for a movie version of *In the Heights*, set for release in 2020. And in July, Miranda announced that he'd created the Flamboyan Arts Fund to help artists and arts organizations in Puerto Rico.

"As someone whose life has been transformed by the power of the arts, and who has witnessed the incredible healing, growth, stability and well being that cultural institutions can bring to local communities, I cannot stand idly by and watch Puerto Rico's arts and culture scene suffer," he said.

At this stage in his life, Miranda's future looks to be full of rich possibilities. He continues his work as an artist, harnessing his passion for telling stories and creating songs. As success propels him forward, he also uses his resources to help others and make a difference in the world he loves.

As he said on his way to visiting the devastation in Puerto Rico, "No shortage of bad news. But also no shortage of ways to do some good."

IMPORTANT DATES

1980 Lin-Manuel Miranda is born on January 16 in New York City.

1992 He begins performing in musical theater in sixth grade at school.

2000 The first performance of Miranda's show *In the Heights* takes place.

2002 He graduates from Wesleyan University.

2008 *In the Heights* opens on Broadway.

2009 Miranda performs "Alexander Hamilton," his first rap song from the yet-to-be-completed *Hamilton* score, at the White House.

2012 He performs sections of "The Hamilton Mixtape" at Lincoln Center in New York City.

2014 His son Sebastian is born.

2015 *Hamilton* opens on Broadway.

Miranda creates the Hamilton Education Program.

He receives a MacArthur Fellowship.

2016 *Moana*, with Miranda's original songs, is released in theaters.

Hamilton wins eleven Tony Awards.

2017 Miranda's son Francisco is born.

2018 *Mary Poppins Returns*, with Miranda in a leading role, is released in theaters.

Miranda launches the Flamboyan Arts Fund.

2019 He stars in *Hamilton* in Puerto Rico.

2020 His *In the Heights* film is scheduled for release.

INDEX